'Cocaine Shadows'

Foreword

Cocaine Shadows takes you on a journey of the life of Roscoe Copeland beginning with his Father and Mother's early life and the love and potpourri times of his mother's pregnancy, and his eventual birth.

The book is a coming of age tale of urban life, much like J. D. Salinger's iconic character Holden Caulfield, from "*The Catcher in the Rye.*" Copeland has the same coming of age experiences as Caulfield, teenage angst and alienation, while dealing with the complex issues of identity, belonging, loss and connection.

Copeland's tale is woven however from the cloth of the urban malaise, that dark place in our country that none dares speak to or of. However this dark place does exist and Copeland speaks to it and of it brilliantly with a bit of chaser for those that do not believe this world exists.

This is an urban tale one should not forget, for it speaks of redemption for us all.

Ken Sanders
Detroit, Michigan
(October 1, 2015)

COPYRIGHT 2015 •ALL RIGHTS RESERVED
(No part of this book may be reproduced without permission of the Copyright owner)

TABLE OF CONTENTS

Chapter 1 – The Angle

Chapter 2 – Silhouette

Chapter 3 – Touching the Surface

Chapter 4 – Reverse Projection

Chapter 5 – Positive Dynamics

Chapter 6 – Dark Images

Chapter 7 - Distance

COPYRIGHT 2015 •ALL RIGHTS RESERVED
(No part of this book may be reproduced without permission of the Copyright owner)

Chapter 1
The Angle

It was the middle of the first semester at Burroughs Middle School in Detroit, MI. A young man named Roscoe had the students laughing and in an uproar at the jokes he made about several of their classmates. The more the teacher tried to regain power over the class the funnier his jokes would become. It suddenly went silent as the big wooden door squeaked open. Everyone thought it was the school's principal coming to see what all the noise was about.

However, the doors opened and a brown skin, slender young man entered the room. He looked somewhat nervous and walked very slowly while glancing through the classroom. As he made his way towards the teachers desk to hand her his note; Roscoe said, "Who is this nigga"? All the students began laughing and pointing at the young man. Then the teacher introduced him. "Class this is our new student, his name is Moses", she said while showing him a chair in the back for him to take a seat. "Moses! Like that dude the preachers be talking about in the bible"? Roscoe asked. Then he stood up on his chair and said, "Hey yawl! This kid knows how to part the red sea". All the students began laughing louder. "Fuck you", Moses yelled as he stared at Roscoe intensely. "Hold on young nigga! Who the fuck you think you talking to like that", Roscoe shouted while jumping off the chair. One of the other students quickly got out her seat and stopped Roscoe from coming near to Moses. Her name was Emma. "Just let it go", she said. So Roscoe began slowly walking back to his seat.

Everyone thought that things were going to be calm, but no sooner than they thought it; this black history class turned more chaotic. Before Roscoe could take his seat, some guys ran into the classroom to fight him.

They didn't ask any questions but ran up on Roscoe so fast and began punching and kicking. However, this was nothing new to Roscoe he was use to fighting more than one person at a time. He tried to fight them off as long as he could but there were just too many of them. They were members of three different gangs. They called themselves 'the Bishops', 'the BKs' which stood for Black Killas and the Chain Gang. All three were well known around the city and most people were afraid when they came around, so none of the students dared to help Roscoe fight. Some of the gang bangers stood there with their guns drawn, just in case someone tried to jump in. There were chairs, trash cans and books flying everywhere. Eventually, Roscoe ran out of the classroom to get away from them as they pursued him, but he lost them.

Moses watched as the students began helping the teacher get the classroom back in order. He could tell from their reaction and comments that although Roscoe was certainly a bad boy, everyone liked him. "I hope he is ok", Emma said as one of the other girls came and hugged her.

Roscoe stayed out of school for about a week. When he came back the following Thursday; he acted as if the fight that took place in black history class had never happened. As he went down the hallway he saw Moses coming towards him. "Hey you're the new boy right"? Roscoe asked as they met towards the auditorium. "Yea", Moses replied while balling up his fist expecting a fight to jump off. "Hold on, it's cool", Roscoe stated upon seeing that Moses had become defensive. "I just wanted to say that I noticed you were in the neighborhood over the weekend, how long have you lived on Vandyke?" he asked. "We just moved in this area", Moses replied. "Well you're gonna need some niggas that got your back, so you can hang with us", Roscoe stated while him and some other older boys headed towards the science lab on the south side of the building.

The bell rang and the halls were becoming empty quick. Everyone rushed inside the classrooms so that they wouldn't be late. However, Roscoe was not at all moved by the rules or school regulations. He was his own man, full of so much street knowledge at such a young age. Hour after hour, he and his friends would stand around in the back hallways of the middle school, contemplating on how they were going to make money. They felt as though school was unnecessary and had no interest in taking the route that adults tried to pound in their brains. Now Roscoe was not very tall. He had an athletic build, dark complexion skin and a confidence about himself that made him irresistible to the young ladies.

However, it was only one young lady that had his full attention. She was a very smart straight 'A' student that kept to herself. She would hang around a very small group of her peers that were like minded, but there was something about her that made her stand out from the rest. No one knew how much Roscoe really liked Kelly and he would never fully express it.

Kelly was the type of girl that a boy would have to come correct to strike her interest. He wouldn't be able to approach her in any ole type of manner. Kelly had very over protective parents and was raised to focus on school first and male friends last. But Roscoe did not care. He knew he wanted her to be his girlfriend and he just had to come up with an angle that would be beneficial to him but not taint his reputation of being one of the toughest guys in school. He couldn't risk the chances of other people thinking for one second that he was soft, an undercover romantic and absolutely leveled by the beauty, IQ and mature qualities found in a girl.

Finally, one day as Roscoe laid on his twin sized bed, meditating on the type of life he wanted to live he decided that he would make his move. On Monday, when school was back in session, he would tell Kelly how, she would be his.

The last day of the week was what Roscoe called his, "freaky Fridays". He would ditch school along with some of his friends to meet up at his house. Once his mother would leave to go to work at the fish store Roscoe would sneak some of the guys and girls from school into the house, through his bedroom window. They would sit around and smoke weed, play cards, have sex and party as if they were adults.

Over the weekend, his friends stopped by the house as normal. They were ready to hit the streets of Detroit. The boys would always have fun times when they were around one another. However, some sort of mischief would always be in the plan for the day. They had a mentality that in order to make it out in the world, it was killed or be killed. Saturday was just a day for the boys to chill. The regular crew of girls, who were invited to the house on Friday did not hang with the fellas on Saturday. This was their time to get out and meet new people and do only what guys were meant to do. Nobody ever understood what caused these young men to have this mind set, but they understood one another and looked after each other as if they were brothers. Moses was along-side Roscoe as they walk in the Van Dyke Avenue neighborhood. Drug addicts stopped them and bought marijuana, pills and other types of stimulants.

The guys decided to stop by the corner store to buy a few snacks. They had planned to go back to Moses house to chill since he was the new guy. Upon them coming out of the store some other young men were coming down the block. All of a sudden; Roscoe took off running. His friends looked at one another, trying to figure out what made him just scatter so quickly. As they ran behind him, they were all laughing and convinced that Roscoe must have smoked too much weed. But they weren't nearly prepared for what their eyes were about to behold. As they went into the back alley way behind the store that Roscoe ran down, he was nowhere in sight. Moses then yelled out, "Look!" as he pointed upward.

Roscoe had climbed onto the roof of the school across the street and was still running, then right before their eyes he jumped off. The boys ran frantically towards where he landed. They just knew he would be seriously hurt or have broken bones, but to their surprise Roscoe was fine and steadily walking at fast pace towards home. Once the guys caught up with him, they were laughing hysterically. They told him that he couldn't have any more weed if he was going to react in this manner after smoking. Roscoe laughed with them as they continued to go towards Moses house.

Later that night, Roscoe sat in his room and thought about the course of events that had taken place. He wondered if his friends would ever realize that he wasn't blown off marijuana. He wasn't running because he was high. Drugs did not make him climb or leap off the building, but fear did. What his friends were not aware of, was that Roscoe was in multiple gangs and the other young men who were coming down the block when they stepped out the store, were in a rival gang, but Roscoe was a member of both. Something like this would be looked at as betrayal and un-loyal. But before Roscoe joined either gang, he had friends and family on both sides, which made it hard for him to say no, when asked to be a part of either. He decided to stay in the house for the remainder of the weekend, to avoid getting into any trouble.

On Monday morning Roscoe was dressed and ready for school earlier than normal. His mother noticed the change but didn't say anything as he left out the door. His purpose for being in school on this day was very clear and simple. To make sure Kelly knew that she deserved and owed it to herself to be his girl. As he stood with his friends in the hallway, the bell rang for third hour classes to be dismissed. Once the students began to fill the well-lit hallways, Roscoe, Moses and the other guys began to walk towards the gymnasium, which would be the next class that Kelly would be headed to.

Kelly stopped at her locker to put her books away and grab her clothes for gym. As her and the other girls stood laughing and conversing of their plans for after school, Kelly caught a glimpse of Roscoe coming down the hall wearing all black. He was truly handsome and secretly she had a crush on him, but knew her parents were not going to allow her to date until she was well off in high school maybe. Also; Roscoe was not the type of guy that her parents would approve of. He was a gang banger that stayed in a lot of trouble and thought school to be a joke. As Kelly, gathered all her things and closed her locker, there Roscoe stood with all his boys surrounding the girls.

"Hey Beautiful", he said to Kelly in a nice calm voice. Her heart nearly melted but she was too proud to allow anyone to see it. Instead, Kelly confidently spoke back and pardoned her way through the crowd. "Can I talk to you for a minute", Roscoe yelled. But Kelly ignored him and kept walking and laughing down the hall with her friends. One of her friends asked if she was crazy. This was Roscoe calling out for her. All the girls in the school would kill for a chance to be chosen by him. But Kelly responded by saying she didn't want anything to do with people who were in gangs.

One of Roscoe friends asked if he wanted him to go and grab her up, but Roscoe was not in to making a big scene when it came to matters of the heart. "No, she'll be mines! Yawl knows I get what I want", he said in low toned voice. For weeks Roscoe would pursue Kelly but seemed as though she would not bend her rules. Until one day she was alone at her locker and his boys were not around. Neither of them had anything to prove to anyone. All guards were totally down and both were vulnerable to give in to how they really felt. So once again, Roscoe approached Kelly. As she slowly stood up from putting her sneakers in the bottom of her locker, to her surprise there Roscoe stood. There was something different about him this time. Kelly saw sincerity in his eyes that had not been there previously. For the first time, she saw the real him. So this time she was compelled to stop and engage in a conversation. To her surprise and contrary to popular belief, he was very well mannered and spoke more intelligently than most. Kelly became quickly intrigued with his personality. Deep down, she really did like Roscoe and he undoubtedly liked her in return, so they ended the conversation with the exchange of telephone numbers.

Once school let out Kelly built up enough courage to ask her parents if she could have boy phone calls. After all;

she would be in high school soon and had proven that she was mature enough to make reasonable decisions. To her surprise, her parents agreed. From that day, Roscoe and Kelly began spending endless hours talking on the telephone and getting to know each other better. Kelly would often try to persuade Roscoe to get out the lifestyle of gang banging. She would constantly compliment him on his witty personality and millionaire imagination. Kelly understood that the qualities that were inside of him just needed to be unveiled cultivated and loved. However, Roscoe would listen to Kelly, but he did not ever see himself living without the guys that had become like family to him. Gang banging had become a part of him and he swore he was in it for life. Although they felt differently on a lot of topics, neither of them could deny the fact that they had deep feelings for each other. So after three months of talking on the phone and hanging out, they decided to make it official and began dating. No one could believe it. They were viewed as a true example of a good girl, bad guy relationship. But they didn't care what others thought about them. They continued dating through the end of the year.

Chapter 2
Silhouette

The Van Dyke guys were getting ready to throw their regular weekend party to end the school year. Roscoe was excited about the party being held at Moses house this year. This proved that even though Moses was the newest member of the gang he was definitely a part of their crew. By this time Roscoe and Moses had become the very best of friends and it was nothing they would not do for one another. Moses family didn't like a lot of his friends but for some reason they all were drawn to Roscoe and liked him very much.

Roscoe stopped by early so that him and Moses could go out and buy their personal weed and drinks before the party began. Although they sold marijuana they vowed never to buy from themselves, just as a rule of business. They were excited, but showed class and style as they walked down street dressed alike wearing their Bossalini hats. Suddenly, the police pulled up where they were walking and shined the overhead flashlight in their faces.

"Take them Mutha Fucking hats off", they yelled as the boys continued walking. "Fuck You"! Roscoe yelled back while looking them dead in their eyes. The cops then got out of their car and began to handcuff and grab the boys up. Some other black kids were coming down the street that saw the whole thing. They surrounded the cop car with poles and bats so the officers quickly got out of the area to avoid a riot occurring. The kids that surrounded the car were not afraid of being arrested because everyone knew these particular white officers were a part of what was called the 'stress team'. What they were known for doing, did not align with state procedure and was unlawful. They were off duty, undercover Hippie officers that purposely went about harassing young black children.

One of the kids that came to Roscoe and Moses aide asked where they were headed all dressed up like mob bosses. "We are members of the black aces and will be having a party tonight. It only cost 25 cents to get in, would you all like to come"? Roscoe replied. So they agreed to meet them there.

Once they got back to the house the other members had already began the party. The Black Aces had their party going on in the basement while the adults were upstairs having a card party. Suddenly, there was a loud crash of glass breaking from upstairs. The kids in the basement could hear tussling and cursing as the grown-ups were arguing back and forward. Moses began to tell everyone that the party was over as Roscoe went up to the second level to see what was happening. Moses mom assured Roscoe that everything was okay and that one of the guests just got a little wild because he lost at bid wiz. She went on to tell him that everything was under control. However, the guys thought it would still be best if they just called it a night for the basement party.

Since everything was in an uproar, Moses decided to walk Roscoe back to his house to get out of the environment for a while. "You want to go and get our weed now, since we were so rudely interrupted by the stress team earlier", Roscoe asked, while Moses chuckled while shaking his yes. As the young men traveled down the street, Roscoe began rhyming about the different events that occurred throughout the day. He would do this often as a way to relieve tension, but everyone thought it was hilarious. He would make up rhymes about anything at any given moment. No one ever realized that years later this would be considered as free style hip hop or rap music. All they knew was that Roscoe had a habit of doing it, to break the intense atmosphere and it made people feel more joyful and happy when he did.

Once they reached the brown house the sat in the middle of the block to purchase marijuana. Neither Roscoe nor Moses was nearly prepared for what they were about to see. The door was partially cracked wherein they were able to just push it open. Considering they were pretty cool with the weed guy they decided to just come right in. Once they bent the corner of the entrance they saw six lifeless (two female and four male) bodies lying on the floor in blood. The house was ransacked, dark and had a stench of death in the atmosphere. "Let's go!" Moses said as his voice trembled with fear. "Okay, just let me grab this." Roscoe said while taking items that he felt the police would take anyway once they got there. Finally, the boys hurried out the house as Moses yelled, "Roscoe come on before someone thinks we did this." They could hear the sirens in a distance as they continued towards Roscoe home. The boys began to discuss what they had just encountered.

They had been through a lot together and witnessed a lot of things but never had they saw anything like this. As they got closer to Roscoe house, Moses noticed a deep sigh that Roscoe released upon seeing an older man standing in the doorway.

"Are you okay, who is that man?" Moses asked while staring at the look of distress on Roscoe face. "That's my mom's friend. Nobody knows the hell I'm living in." Roscoe replied as he released another deep sigh. "Tell me what's going on." Moses stated while looking intensely at the young man he had grown to love as a brother. Seeing the sincerity in Moses eyes, Roscoe began to explain what he encountered on a regular basis. "When my mom is not around, this man beats me and ties me up in the basement. I am alone, cold and scared and it feels as though the walls are caving in on me. He told me that if I ever tell her what was happening then he would kill us both". Moses saw a fear in Roscoe eyes that he had never saw before as he finished speaking.

However, Roscoe never wanted to show any vulnerability around anyone so he quickly changed the subject. "Well enough about that", he said abruptly as they reached his porch. "I've been thinking about going to hear Farakan speak on next week at Cobo Hall," he stated. Moses assured him that he would support him in whatever he decided to do. He knew that Roscoe was a great fan of Malcolm X; he did a lot of reading on religion and was seriously thinking of becoming a part of the nation of Islam. Although Moses went along with the conversation, he couldn't help his mind from converting back to what his friend was going through with this man in his mother's life.

Over the summer break, Moses got Roscoe a job working at a gas station in the heart of Detroit, the boys were so excited about making a steady wage of twenty-five cents an hour for pumping gas and checking oil. Then to top it off, because of where the gas station was located (on 12th Ave. and Glynn Rd.) they would always have the opportunity to meet celebrities. One night there was a concert in town and they became very excited at having the opportunity to pump the gas for Aretha Franklin, Marvin Gaye and The Temptations, upon which they received generous tips. Both Roscoe and Moses made the decision that they would save the money they made from working at the gas station and begin having parties on a larger scale or to what some knew as hosting cabarets.

Chapter 3
Touching the Surface

Summer break was awesome. But it was now time for the school year to start. Kelly was excited to begin high school and by this time she and Roscoe had fell in love with one another. Their days and nights were constantly filled with one another's' presence and over the years Kelly saw a change in Roscoe that she knew was there all along. He had begun to mature and take like a little more serious. However, he still ran with his friends from time to time.

As the high school years passed, Roscoe realized he was madly in love with Kelly and had settled in his mind that he would not cheat on her or ever let her go. She was not just his girlfriend but Kelly had become his best friend. There was only one other person that he loved more than Kelly. Her name was Charisma. She was absolutely gorgeous. Every time Roscoe would see her, he knew their bond would be unbreakable and Charisma felt the same way. Whenever Roscoe came over she would run to him as if he was the last man on the planet. As he would hold her in his arms she would gently lay her head on his shoulder to enjoy the sense of love, security and comfort that only a father could give. Charisma was birthed into Roscoe's life three years ago and he still would sit and reminisce about the time she was born. And although he was not allowed to see here in the hospital the day she was born. This child had become his world and no love could compare to what Roscoe felt for Charisma.

Kelly had the opportunity to meet Charisma and she loved her as if she was her own. It was something about her big pretty eyes that would melt the hearts of people that caused them to gravitate towards her. Kelly knew how much Roscoe loved Charisma and she would often pray that his daughter would never be taken away or that he would ever be restricted from seeing him on her account.

Moses witnessed Roscoe being heartbroken as they went over to take Charisma some things that Moses had bought her, but Charisma's grandmother was so upset that her daughter went through with having a child at such a young age and then especially with it being by Roscoe, that she vowed to never allow Roscoe to see the child. She flung open the door and asked what they wanted. Upon

Roscoe explaining to her that he wanted to see Charisma, she disrespectfully slammed the door in their faces. Roscoe would often express to everyone how this was his first child and how he wanted to do right by her.

Then one day as Kelly sat on the front porch reading a book she looked up and saw Roscoe coming towards her house. There was something different she detected as he approached the stairs. This was the first time Kelly saw emotions this intense radiate from Roscoe. He stood there for a moment with his eyes full of tears, with a look of fear, concern and grief. He then came up and embraced Kelly as tight as he possibly could and began to cry. Kelly nervously whispered in his ear, "Baby, what's wrong?" There was a silence in the atmosphere for a moment then finally Roscoe let out a deep sigh and said, "Charisma was hit by a car today and she didn't make it, my baby is gone." Kelly heart dropped as she clutched Roscoe tighter. How would this young man make it pass this point of his life? "You know that God knows best", Kelly said. However, before she could say any more Roscoe stopped her and said, "I know Kelly, I'm not mad with God, but if I had been there my baby would not had been in that street."

After time had passed Roscoe and Kelly had begun babysitting Kelly's niece. She would be with them all the time and Kelly could tell that this little girl being in their life brought a certain relief to Roscoe that was unexplainable. Sometimes they would go to the park and as Kelly would sit on the blanket with her book. She would laugh as she looked up to see her niece running and jumping on Roscoe's back. This child was really what he needed at a time in his life when he thought he would lose his mind from what happened with Charisma.

Roscoe would often just stare and Kelly's niece with the same love and compassion as if she was his daughter. They would buy her toys, gifts, candy and clothes every time they had a chance. Kelly's sister was fine with the love and attention that they gave her daughter. She knew she was at work a lot and couldn't spend as much time with her as was needed. But one day something happened that changed all their lives. Amy (Kelly's Sister) came to pick her daughter up from Roscoe and Kelly who were babysitting. As they were gathering all her stuff that had been bought that day and loading it in Amy's car, the little girl hopped out the car ran up to Kelly hugged her tight and said, "I love you mommy." Kelly could see the hurt in Amy eyes as she explained to her niece that she was her aunt. But later that night Amy called and told Kelly that she didn't think it would be wise to have her and Roscoe baby sit anymore and she thanked them for all they had done. Roscoe was more hurt than Kelly. He had truly grown close to this child and everything about her reminded him of the love he had for Charisma. Now after a year of growing attached to this child, she would be out of their lives too. Kelly could see the sadness in Roscoe's eyes as they lay across the bed and discussed everything that had taken place. So on that night they decided that they wanted to have a child of their own. They both agreed that this child would be a replica of their bond and the love they had for one another. With them planning to have this new addition enter their lives, they then began writing out and brainstorming on ways to ensure they had more than enough finances to care for a baby. After all the planning was completed, they looked at each other and began to laugh. They both knew that they were serious. The love they shared was more intense than ever before. Every touch, every kiss, every embrace was filled with deep passion and on that very night, conception took place.

On the next day Roscoe walked over to Moses house to try and relieve some stress. By this time Moses had moved off Vandyke and now lived in Highland Park which was around a five mile distance. Once Roscoe arrived, Moses mom greeted him at the door and said, "I am glad that you are here maybe you can calm him down." Upon Roscoe entering the back room he noticed Moses sitting on the bed furious. Before Roscoe could ask any questions Moses began to speak. "Dog! I'm telling you if this nigga try and whoop me I'm killing his ass tonight", Moses said while pacing back and forth. "What is going on?" Roscoe asked as he grabbed Moses arm for him to take a seat. However, Moses was too heated to stay still. "He's the one that told me to go take my sister driving, and once she dents his car, he talking bout he gone whoop my ass? I don't think so! It ain't going down like that! I will blow that mutha fucker brains out first. As a matter of fact, I think I will go in there and do it right now, considering this nigga never did anything for me." Moses proclaimed as he grabbed a 357 handgun from under the mattress. Roscoe began to talk Moses out of his angry state of mind. He convinced him to walk with him to the liquor store. "It seems like we're both having a bad day," Roscoe said as they approached their destination. "What do you mean?" Moses asked. "A car hit my baby girl while she was playing in the street and killed her," Roscoe replied.

Suddenly, tears flowed like an uncontrollable flood. Moses watched as Roscoe began questioning the call he felt was made by God. This was the first time Moses witnessed Roscoe in this frail state of vulnerability. His heart went out for his friend, his brother as they walked back towards Moses house.

After a few months had passed Roscoe received a call from Kelly, telling him that their plan had worked and she was now pregnant. He was ecstatic that the woman he loved would soon give him a child that would mend his broken heart. He had all types of jobs to make sure they would have enough money to live well. During that time

Detroit, MI was well known for being a great avenue for the entertainment industry, so Roscoe began his very own company entitled Creative Enterprise. He wrote a play and had plans on taking this company to the top. Moses was concerned that his friend was moving too fast and too quickly. They hadn't even started in Kettering High School yet and Roscoe was already talking about trying to find ways on raising a family and starting a business. He felt as though Roscoe was getting in too deep and way above his age, too far ahead of time. However, Roscoe had a made up mind and began working really hard for several months getting everything perfect for the night of the play. The venue was booked, the cast were enthusiastic and the tickets were sold out. Everyone was excited! Certainly, this path would bring in much wealth and keep Roscoe out of trouble. An hour before the play was to begin, Roscoe began going around the room checking on the cast to make sure everyone was okay. Suddenly, behind him he heard a loud scream from one of the over dramatic cast members that was sitting and talking with Kelly. As Roscoe turned and looked, everyone was standing around like frozen statues. Kelly water broke! And the labor pains had begun.

Roscoe ran frantically over to Kelly and began giving Moses instructions on how to ensure that the night went off without any errors. Roscoe was excited that on this very special night his child was about to be birthed and so was his career. But nothing meant more to him than being there to witness his son come into the world. However, Kelly knew how hard he had worked on the play and she felt that it would be wise if he stayed himself to make sure that everything went perfect. Roscoe re-assured her that he would be on his way right after the play was done and he kept his word. When he arrived at the hospital Kelly laid in the bed with a clear crib beside her. Roscoe walked over slowly, with a dozen of roses and a teddy bear for Kelly.

He gently kissed her on her forehead while giving her the items he had bought and then leaned over to pick up his son out of the crib. Kelly watched as his eyes lit up the whole room. "My Seed", Roscoe whispered softly into the ears of this newborn child that had eyes as gentle as his mother.

A few weeks after leaving the hospital, neither Roscoe nor Kelly wanted to be a burden to their parents so they decided that it was time they had their own place. Roscoe would work day in and day out while Kelly would continually look to find somewhere for them to move. Finally, she was accepted to move into the Jeffries Housing Project near downtown Detroit. Roscoe would have Kelly come to his job and pick up his check, and cash it to give for their first month rent and security deposit. They were pleased with the decision they made to step out on their own, but they realized that having their own apartment and a child meant much more financial obligations than what they expected. However, they weren't overly concerned with this matter because they both had a drive and tenacity to not just dream, but to also pursue what they wanted in life.

Roscoe decided that a regular nine to five job would not be enough so he got with Moses and they decided to begin throwing cabarets regularly at a space that a man rented to them with no questions asked. The owner did not care about their age or where they got the money from. As long as they had enough to cover the rental cost and they didn't destroy his property, he was fine with them renting the space. Once they saw that this partnership was good they began to rent the space for more activities. It went from cabarets to parties and then fashion shows. This really began to change the outlook on a lot of things. More people begin to hear about what Roscoe had going on; and they wanted to become involved. Many beautiful women would come and audition to be in the fashion shows which really began to challenge the authenticity of Roscoe and Kelly's relationship. The even more intriguing part was that they had attended school with a girl named Alicia Myers who had become famous for her singing and would come and perform occasionally at their events.

One day things really became heated as a new girl entered the office to interview to become a model for the fashion show. Both Kelly and Moses could tell that Roscoe was intrigued by this woman's beauty as he smiled at her every word and gesture. You could see the jealousy in Kelly's face as her man stared intensely in the eyes of this other woman. Without any input or second guessing Roscoe told her that she was hired to be a part of the show.

Kelly politely walked out the room without ever saying a word.

Chapter 4
Reverse Projection

One day when Roscoe came home from work, he quietly stood in the entrance of the living room and leaned against the wall watching as Kelly sat there with their son, Scoe on her lap and began reading to him. Although he was only a baby it was an amazing experience that Roscoe loved to watch how his son interacted as if he understood everything that was going on. Kelly looked up and realized Roscoe was standing there watching them. She gave a warm smile and continued reading.

That night Roscoe and Kelly lie in bed and began talking about everything they had been through. He told her that he felt the exact same way he had felt 10 yrs. ago when he first met her in middle school. He went on to say that he could not imagine ever having a life without her and little Scoe in it. Then Roscoe reached in his coat pocket and pulled out the small black box that every woman waits to see from the man that they love. "Marry Me," he said while staring lovingly at Kelly; and without hesitation, "Of course!" Kelly replied as they embraced.

After the wedding their family really began growing. Over the years six children were added to comprise their family tree. Roscoe and Kelly was more in love than they had ever been. However, money was really beginning to get tight and they wanted their children to have the best of everything. They began making plans to send all their children to college if they so desired. Although it seemed as though there was never quite enough to save, they vowed never to veer from the plan.

One day Kelly went to see her Mother-in-law. They always got along, and Roscoe mom loved Kelly as if she was her very own daughter. As they sat at the table talking she smiled at Kelly and said, "I have something for you", while leaving the room. Kelly sat wondering what she could possibly have while waiting for her to return. "I don't want you to raise my grandchildren up in the projects, so you all can have a house that I own", she said while handing Kelly a set of keys. Kelly was ecstatic. She couldn't believe the generosity that her Mother-in-law had shown and she couldn't wait to tell Roscoe and the children.

Once the children began getting older, Kelly really began to buckle down with them to ensure that they would be smart and make it through school with good grades. Therefore, every day after they came home from regular school, they had a regular routine of first doing their homework and then sit in with her for home schooling sessions.

Roscoe was away from the house a lot, trying to hustle up on money by running the multiple business ventures to make sure everything stayed afloat. However, Kelly didn't like the idea of him being away from the house so much and especially with the temptations of other women being a weak point in his life. Scoe could see that his mother was overwhelmed from time to time so he took the initiative as the oldest child to help her with the things that were needed around the house. Within a few months so many responsibilities began to be placed on his shoulders at such a young age that many considered him to be the man of the house. One day when Roscoe came home very late, he sat on the sofa and watched as his seven year old son helped Kelly cook, change diapers, prepared bottles, fed, burped and put babies asleep.

Later that night, Scoe lie awake on his bed and listened as his father argued with his mother about having him doing all these things. "My son is going to be a strong entrepreneur like me! Not some damn home maker," Roscoe yelled. "What do you expect me to do? I need help around here and you're never home," Kelly griped back. "I am out here trying to make sure we have food on the table and can pay these bills!" Roscoe replied. "Oh and don't forget cheating on your wife and paying God knows whoever else bills," Kelly said while leaving their bedroom and heading down stairs. Scoe could still hear their voices faintly in the night air as his dad followed his mom to the lower level. Eventually he drifted off to sleep. Suddenly, he jumped up in the middle of the night as if he had a nightmare. While sitting on his twin sized bed staring off into the ceiling he began to hear a gentle whimpering noise coming down the hallway. As he wiped the sleep from his eyes and released a soft yawn, he quietly climbed out the bed and proceeded down the hallway. The house was very dark besides the one night light that Kelly would have plugged in the bathroom for the sake of the children. The only sound you could hear was the small footsteps of this young child as he headed towards his parents room in his blue superman pajamas. As he gently pushed the door open he noticed that his father wasn't there. His mother lied there clutching the satin pink pillow in a gloomy moonlit room. "Ma, what's wrong", he spoke as his tiny voice caused her to quickly try and gather her emotions so that she wouldn't frighten him. "Baby what are you doing awake?" she said in a still, calm tone. "I heard a noise so I came to see what was going on," Scoe replied as he jumped onto her bed and falling upon her arm. Suddenly, Kelly released the sound of excruciating pain. Realizing that his mother was hurt caused this fragile child to experience heartbreak for the first time in his life. His eyes became filled with tears that displayed a love so pure and tender that it caused Kelly to cry as well. That night Scoe would lie on the pillow next to his mother and softly rubbed her arm until she fell asleep. From that night, Scoe began to look at his father differently. He still loved him and had respect for him, but he didn't want to ever think of anyone hurting his mother again.

For weeks, it was hard for Scoe to concentrate in school. He would normally be very attentive in class, but considering the school sat a field away from their house, he couldn't help but stare out the window each day. He watched to see if the police would be called for his parents fighting or if an ambulance would one day come to pick up his mother. The things that consumed the mind of this young boy, is what some would consider torture. However, it was all he could think of until the bell rang. One day, he was kicked out of school and had to come home early. As he came into the house there was a stench in the air as if he had just entered a sports arena. Upon coming closer towards the living room he could hear his father yelling as his mother sat there and cried. "Please, don't cry mom," Scoe yelled as he dropped his books, ran across the room and embraced her. As usual, Kelly tried to pull herself together for the sake of her child but the next statements gave her the worst verbal blow ever. "You have ruined my chances of becoming the best swimmer ever, because of what you did to my arm," she yelled. "Let me enlighten you on something, they were never going to allow a black woman to swim in the Olympics anyway so give it up," he screamed. Kelly could not hold it together any longer, she began to cry harder than Scoe or his dad had ever heard before. This was the worst feeling in the world for this boy to watch his mother heartbroken and dreams trampled on as if they were nothing. It was like with every tear that dropped from Kelly's face caused Scoe's heart to skip a beat. "Leave her alone daddy, just leave her alone," he said a second time even louder. "Now look at what you're doing, you've turned my son against me," Roscoe said as he shook his head, grabbed his coat and left.

    Scoe began to clean up some of the mess that was thrown all over the house from the fight, so the other children wouldn't witness it once they came home. Kelly began to fix them a meal. As the other children arrived from school they came in smiling and laughing unaware as what had just happened. "Put your things away and come eat a little something, then you guys can go outside and play for a while", Kelly stated while stirring a pot of hotdogs and pork n beans. The kids were shocked. Normally they had to home school before being able to play but nobody asked any questions, they just quickly ate and ran outside. However, Scoe stayed in this day. He watched as his mother face would display pain every time she went to lift the pot off the stove. Therefore, he went into the kitchen and began to put away the leftovers and washed the dishes so that Kelly could relax. Now, at this time his youngest sister was still an infant. So whenever she would cry, needed to fed, picked up or put to sleep, Scoe would have to do it for Kelly. The weight of the baby was too much for Kelly to bear and she didn't want to risk the chance of dropping her. Scoe would hold her as if she was his child and bounce while pacing the floor until she would fall asleep.

As time moved on Scoe had become so use to being the man of the house and taking care of things that it was natural instincts for him to be protective of his brothers and sisters and even his mother. Kelly always knew that she was robbing him of his childhood, but he was the only help that she had and she needed him to be her strength to carry on. However, one day as he began his normal routine of making sure the baby was ok, trying to figure out what he was going to make for the other kids to eat and concentrating on his homework, Kelly observed the tasks that had been placed on him. Once, Scoe finished preparing everything he sat by the window to look out at his other siblings playing and to make sure they were okay. During this time he thought about how he really didn't like going to church, but how Kelly would make them go. He felt like God had left them to fend for themselves and really didn't care about them. He looked and saw the children from down the block as they rode their bikes, had the newest gym shoes and clothes and were admired by all the other kids. He began to ask God why did it seem like everyone else was doing so good, having a great Christmas, and they were struggling. He remembered how when he was little and his dad worked by doing plays and cabarets, how they had anything they wanted and everyone seemed happy. What had changed? Why were things so different? How did they get to this low place? As he continued to stare into the sky from the window his mind began to drift to what he heard the preacher say about, "holding on and having faith". Therefore, he equated that message to be a revelation to what he and his family were going through, and that day in his heart he began to believe that God would eventually make things better. Kelly noticed how deep in thought Scoe was and gently came over and assured him that she had everything handled inside the house and for him to go outside and play.

 Now Scoe was a very smart and intuitive child. When it came to his personality he had the hustle and drive of his father in him along with the intelligence of his mother. Therefore, schoolwork came easy. However, due to the fact that he seldom got the chance to be outdoors and play, when he was afforded that opportunity it was like unleashing a wild animal. He would find all sorts of mischief to get into, but also loved playing football with some of the kids on the block. However once he came in the alleyway where the other children were, he noticed that one of the boy's name Mark was about to fight his brother, so Scoe stepped in and he and Mark began fighting. Later they became the best of friends and could always be found hanging out together.

Chapter 5
Positive Dynamics

As the years went on, Scoe was beginning to really enjoy the freedom of getting out of the house more often. He would find different things to get involved in just so he could have what he felt would be a normal childhood like everyone else. His youngest sister wasn't a baby any more, therefore, he no longer had the responsibility of changing diapers, making bottles or pacing the floor all night to put her asleep. He began to think that this would make things less stressful but however, he could not be more wrong. With Roscoe never being at home much and just coming and going as he pleased, the burden was placed in Scoe's hand to try to do everything he could in order to bring money into the house. He was barely a teenager, and now his big brother duties had shifted into becoming the man of the house and the father figure.

One day as he sat on the front porch of their house, he began to think about how things were when he was much younger. He missed the days when they had enough money to do whatever they pleased. He thought about how as a child, he watched his dad single handedly run three to four business at a time. His fondest memory caused him to begin smiling as he reminisced. When he was only five years old his parents owned a store that brought in many customers daily. Roscoe would have to go and check on the other businesses so he taught Scoe and his slightly younger brother how to run the business in the front of the store while Kelly tended to customers that visited her Boutique in the back of the store. Truly this was a family business and Scoe was always eager to go to work even at a young age. New customers would always be surprised to see this child behind the cash register handling making transactions, giving the correct amount of change as well as professional customer service. He thought about how the store sat across from Cooper School and how many of the children who attended there, would come in to play pac-man and pinball after purchasing their penny candy.

"Wow," he whispered softly to himself. Then sadness came across his face. His thoughts began to run wild. What went wrong, how did they end up from having everything to barely having enough to make ends meet? As he stared off into the clouds that gently moved across the big blue sky it began to come in clear. How could he have forgotten what caused everything to begin sliding downhill? It all happened at the store.

It was a warm summer evening in Detroit. Kelly and Scoe had been in the store and boutique all day and were tired and ready to go home. Roscoe had come to see how business went that day, because he had been held up at the other business. He was very well known in the neighborhood and had purchased Cooley Lounge where people came in to have a relaxed time and shot pool. After watching his mom and dad discuss the monies that had accumulated that day, Kelly and Scoe proceeded to leave to go home. "Go ahead and I will be there shortly," Roscoe said as they left. Scoe remembered how they made it home and before Kelly could sit her purse down, a strange look came across her face. As she began getting dinner out the fridge she suddenly turned to Scoe and said, start preparing dinner and watch your brothers and sisters, I'll be right back. It seemed as though Kelly had been gone for hours. Scoe had finished preparing dinner, made sure his siblings were fed, bathed and in bed before his parents along with Moses (who was both his dad's best friend and Scoe's godfather) made it back to the house.

As he continued to sit on the wooden steps of the porch and stare even more intensely into the sky, thoughts of that night became clearer. Scoe remembered how his dad managed to hurt two of the most important people in his life at the same time. He remembered how he was awakened that night upon hearing the front door slam shut. "How could you do that?" Kelly yelled. "It was a mistake, it was nothing! Don't let this come between us." Roscoe tried to explain. "It's not what you think," he added as Kelly became furious. "Not what I think! Not what I think!" she screamed a second time. "I caught you red handed, fucking that hoe in my boutique, right after telling me and your son you were on your way home. Telling us to go ahead, all while plotting to bring some trash into our family business. Yea, you right Roscoe! It's not what I think; it's what I saw with my own two eyes and it's what I know!" Kelly yelled as she stormed away to the bedroom. Although Roscoe felt bad that he had hurt Kelly, the words of his best friend Moses made him feel the pain even more. "Man! I can't believe you did that," Moses said while looking Roscoe straight in the eyes. "You knew that was my girl and how much I liked her. How can you be so heartless? I don't know that I can forgive you for this one. I mean after all you have Kelly who is all you ever wanted through school, she's an awesome wife and mother, faithful to you and everything. You have her; you have been several of the pretty models at the shows and can basically have any other woman you want. Why would you go after the one who your best friend is dating?" Moses then slammed the front door upon leaving. Scoe remembered how that night changed the family bond that had been built and seemingly glued their good fortunes together. It all began going downhill after that night.

Suddenly, he was awakened from his day dream as his best friend Mark walked up. "What you doing Scoe? It's almost time come on," he said as the two boys headed towards the back of the house. They were preparing to have a show in the back yard of the house and charge people to come in order to make money. This part of his childhood he embraced wholeheartedly. Scoe had learned how to be a hustler since he worked in the store at five years old. He saw the level of respect and commitment that came when money transactions were being made, and from that point desired success in a way that most children don't dream about until they're in college. However, hosting the shows in the back yard along with his best friend was only one of the ways that Scoe was beginning to walk in the shadowed footprints of his father. Because the other children could easily recognize that Scoe was a natural born leader, they asked him to be in charge of the group they had formed on the block. He enjoyed the prestige and attention that he received but his mind remained constantly on how he was going to take care of his family.

Early the next morning Scoe awoke took his shower, brushed his teeth, got dressed and then went downstairs to begin preparing breakfast for his siblings. As the food was simmering he grabbed his box full of change that he had been saving from hosting the shows in the backyard. He also had money that he had saved from helping people with their groceries at the market and pumping people gas.

These were just a few things he hustled and did over the summer to try and build enough to help his mom buy things for the house. However, as he sat their counting the money his countenance changed from joy to sadness as he realized it still was not enough. Then there was a knock at the door. Kelly was up and was going to the door as Scoe was coming out of the kitchen. As she opened the door it was the paperboy, coming to collect his weekly fee. Scoe watched as his mother handed him the money and closed the door. "What are you cooking?" she asked as she headed towards the kitchen. However, Scoe was compelled to go onto the front porch. He watched as the paperboy went from house to house collecting money. "Perfect", he whispered under his breath. "I will become a paperboy and make enough money to really help my mom and family". He didn't tell anyone what he was planning to do. He just knew it had to be done.

The next week he sat on the porch and waited for the paperboy to come deliver the paper. As he made it to where Scoe lived, he stopped the young man and asked him how he could get a job being a paperboy. The young man ignored the question and kept delivering the papers. However, this did not discourage Scoe one bit. He would ask various people while playing outside, until one of the older boys on the block told him how easy it was and exactly where he could go to sign up. Once Scoe heard the location was near Van Dyke Ave. and Grimnell, which were only minutes from where he lived. He decided to go right then and see if he would be hired. Sure enough the man trained and hired him right on the spot. It was beginning to get dark so Scoe rushed home to beat the street lights from coming on. Once he made it home he noticed that his dad was there. It had been a couple of days since Roscoe had been there and the children were very happy to see him.

But Scoe and Kelly just occasionally glanced at one another, wondering if he was going to remain cool all night or cause drama. As everyone sat eating dinner, Scoe decided to share his good news. "I am a paper boy now, I start on Monday," he said aloud while smiling at mother. "I'm proud of you," Kelly said while gently touching his right hand. "That's good son, you get that hustling from me," Roscoe stated as he continued to eat dinner.

Weeks had gone by and Scoe was doing very well working his new job. He enjoyed being the paperboy because it brought much more money into the house. He could tell that it was slowly lifting some of the burden off Kelly and that made him happy. Suddenly, one week as he was making his weekly rounds of picking up subscriptions, delivering papers and collecting money, he noticed a group of guys standing at the end of the block, watching him. By the time he made it to the third block his street smarts and intuition was enlightened. Scoe knew that these guys were waiting for him to finish so that they could rob him. He pondered for a brief moment rather they would kill him, but then that thought quickly disappeared and he knew they only wanted his money. Therefore, begin to think of a smart way to not get into a confrontation with these guys, yet still not come up holding the short end of the stick. Once he went to one of the houses that were angled wherein the guys could not see him, he began separating the money. He took some of the dollar bills and crumbled them in one pocket to make it look like a lot of money. He then put the rest of the dollars along with the bigger bills that he would keep, in his other pocket. As he continued to a couple of more houses the older boys decided to make their move. Once Scoe saw them approaching he was a little nervous. He hoped they didn't have a gun or knife, but either way he was ready for what he knew was about to happen. Upon reaching the end of the block and being face to face with these three guys, Scoe realized one of them (he didn't know him by name) went to the same school as he did. He also knew the other older boys (Scrooge and Tone Cox) by name only from having a reputation for doing this type of stuff around the neighborhood. Scrooge stood there looking angrily at Scoe as Tone yelled, "Give us your money lil nigga." While he was speaking, the boy Scoe had seen around school pulled out a gun. However, Scoe was still focused on his plan and reached in his left pocket to pull out the scrunched up dollars bills. The boys were so excited to see what they thought was a lot of money that they quickly snatched it out of his hands and ran off. Surprisingly, Scoe was not shaken up one bit. He kinda snickered to himself, and his continued to do his weekly routine of going to Burger King after collecting his money to buy a Whopper and Milkshake. However, once he finished eating his meal, he hurried home, in hopes that the guys were not canvasing the area looking for him, after realizing they had not gotten a lot of cash. Once he made it home, he told his mom and dad what happened. "However, I kept the big bucks to help you out mom," he said while handing Kelly some of his money. Roscoe had no remorse as to everything that had taken place. Nor did he feel inadequate at the fact that his son was giving up his hard earned money to provide the household that he should have been providing for. At seeing that Scoe had money left over, Roscoe boldly said, "Son let me borrow this right here," while snatching some of the money out of Scoe's hand. "I'll pay you back," he added while leaving out the front door. Needless to say, Scoe never saw that money again.

 Kelly was a little nervous about Scoe continuing with the paper route, due to the robbery. So he decided to quit. Once again Scoe began to feel the burden of his childhood being swept away. He could never go skating or swimming with his friends because he had a strict schedule that he had to obey. After school he had to do his homework, then home school lessons that Kelly prepared, chores, forty-five minutes outside to play. Scoe knew in the back of his mind that Kelly was just being over protected and raising him and her siblings the best way she knew how, but he often wished that Roscoe would step up and be the father he once was. He believed this would give him a lot more freedom but it seemed as though it wasn't happening quick enough. With him not working the paper route any more, he began to convert back to being in the house all the time and making sure his siblings were okay. Later within the year, Scoe decided that he would join the football team. This would give him a way out of the house. This would be a way for him to channel his anger and frustration. Like everything else that he put his hands to do, he flourished in this area. He was not only good at the sport but began developing a passion for it. Everyone would always tell him how great of a player he was and how he had the potential to play for the NFL one day. The coaches began to watch him closely and Scoe quickly rose to be the star of the team. However, even with the praise and accolades that he received from others, there was sadness in his heart because neither Kelly nor Roscoe ever came to any of his games. He always hoped to one day see at least one of them on the sideline benches cheering him on, but it never happened. Resentment began to build up inside of him that desired to be released. He was mad at his dad for leaving them in a situation that caused for him to become a man before his time. He was upset with his mother because he felt that she had put too much weight on him to bear and his childhood had been stripped. Yet although, he felt as though he didn't have any support from those that he did everything in his world to try and help, he never stayed upset with his mother. Deep down he felt that the way she was raising him with the demands and all, were only meant to build up and pull out greatness. But regardless to the future revelation that Scoe would receive, his current situation caused him to be mad at the world, and he found himself just wanting to play football. He would get awesome grades in school, but his citizenship was very poor, due to having to stay at home and help out or having days when he just didn't want to attend.

Chapter 6
Dark Images

Over the summer new people moved in down the street. However, by this time Scoe and Mark was running their block and all the kids listened to what they said. Both of them were very angry at life and would some days randomly find people to fight for no reason. One day as one of the new boys rode his bike down the street he said something smart and Mark heard him. Now, Scoe was very bitter, but Mark anger was on an entirely different level.

As the new boy came back towards his house, Scoe and Mark caught him in the alley way where all the kids would often play. When the other children saw them come into the alley way; they knew it was about to be trouble; so they quickly began moving over to the sides closer to the houses. Once the new boy came in the area, Scoe and Mark began fighting him. They were punching and kicking him without showing any mercy. Suddenly, Mark did something that even Scoe couldn't believe. He went over and grabbed a piece of broken glass, lodged it in the grooves of his sneakers and kicked the boy in his knee.

Blood began gushing out as the boy ran home crying with his knee busted open. Scoe could tell the other kids were terrified and even he wondered where Mark came up with the thought to do something like that. However he didn't ask any questions as the two of them laughed while walking back to the front of the house.

Meanwhile, Roscoe was not doing well at all. Times had certainly changed for the worst and this intelligent, creative, hustling entrepreneur had gotten caught up with the lifestyle of the world to the point where it was destroying him. By this time Roscoe had made up with Moses and their friendship was back to normal. One late Friday evening, Roscoe stopped by so that they could do their usual weekend routine of getting high and partying. Upon Moses letting Roscoe into the house began to inform him that he already had the marijuana papers and the drinks. "Do you have the weed?" Moses said as he began separating the Top papers to roll the marijuana in. "No, that's kid stuff and we are grown men. It's time to take it to the next phase," Roscoe replied as he pulled out a large pipe with a screen attached. "What the hell is that?" Moses asked while laughing. "It's called crack cocaine," Roscoe stated while pulling out hangers, cotton and a lot of other substances. Roscoe went on saying, "This is the new wave that has hit the streets, everybody is into this now and it gets you high quicker. I have been doing this for months now and I swear to you sometimes I believe I'm flying." Moses was intrigued by the way Roscoe was describing this new drug that had made its way to the streets of Detroit and he trusted the judgment of his best friend so he was willing to give it a try. Moses felt a little weird at first; then he began seeing everything that Roscoe had described. Whenever they got high together, this was their new drug of choice and it made them feel invincible. However, Moses began noticing a change in Roscoe's behavior. First he became fascinated by the Richard Pryor story and how the entertainer still survived after setting himself on fire. Then he began distancing himself from being around Moses and solely had his eyes and life centered on the pipe and getting high.

One night all the fellas gathered up at Roscoe house to play poker with Pope who was a big named drug dealer during that time. As they were all getting high it was a little too much for Moses and when he went to stand up, he lost balance and fell through the table. Roscoe became nervous at first and didn't want his best friend to be hurt, but he didn't want Pope or the other guys to think he was compassionate so they all began laughing and he had some of the guys help him take Moses down the street to his mother's house.

Upon hearing the loud crash, Kelly came down stairs where the men where partying. She patiently waited until Roscoe got back and then pulled him to the side. "I have kids, and you should know better than to be doing all this childish nonsense in our house." She whispered while staring angrily in Roscoe eyes. He could tell that if he didn't do something to clear house right away, then Kelly would do it for him. Certainly, she did not play when it came to the things that influenced the morality of her children. After everyone left, Roscoe was embarrassed and upset. He and Kelly began arguing as if they were two strangers on the street. Name calling and profanity flowed from both their lips without hesitation. Scoe was awakened by the noise and came where they were to try and bring peace to the situation. "Dad, just leave her alone," he said in a calm voice that crackled as he witness the tears rolling down his mother's face. Roscoe could see the hurt that he was causing his family and decided to go for a walk to try and relax.

Once he made it back to the house, Scoe and Kelly were in their rooms but both of them were wide awake. Scoe listened as his dad crept up the stairs trying not to awaken the whole house. He tried to listen to what his dad was saying to Kelly but both their voices were faint in the night distance and sounded so soothing that eventually he could no longer keep his eyes open and fell asleep. Kelly knew that Roscoe had gotten caught up with the new drug that was out, but she wasn't expecting Roscoe to confess the way he did. "Baby, I don't know what to do anymore.

I thought I had a handle on this thing but it has gotten a hold of me and I can't control it." Roscoe explained with tears in his eyes. He went on to say, "every time I decide that I am not going to have today, it's like it calls out to me, I long for it, thirst for it and I can't shake it." By this time tears began to roll down his face. Kelly had not seen this side of her husband in years. She could sense his desire to be free from this drug yet at the same time knew that it had just as much influence over his life that she had. "They have rehab centers," she replied. But Roscoe did not want to be labeled as a person that appeared to be a weakling or as someone who needed the help of others simply to stop using drugs. He felt like he could do it without any help. "No! I will stop," he said in a mellow tone as he curled up in the bed next to Kelly, laid his head on her lap and drifted off to sleep.

Weeks had gone by and Roscoe still had not stopped using the drugs. Things were getting really bad. He would stay out all night and was relentlessly having affairs with multiple women. For days at a time, neither Kelly nor Moses knew where he was and would always hope and pray that he was okay. Eventually he would pop back up, get something to eat, maybe sleep and then out again. After months of this patterned routine, Kelly was fed up. "I'm tire of your shit Roscoe," she yelled as he entered the house. "Don't start woman," he replied as he blew pass her as if what she was feeling didn't matter to him. However, Kelly went on to express her anger. "You staying out all night lying up with God knows who, then coming back here thinking you gone lay in my bed, you got another thang coming. Mama ain't raised no fool."

Suddenly, Roscoe stopped and looked at her with rage in his eyes. "What the hell are you talking about," he yelled. "You my wife, which means your ass belongs to me! Got it! End of got damn story!" His words gripped Kelly spirit in a way that made her furious. She quickly rose to her feet, stood in his face and said, "NO! I'm not your wife, that hoe down the street that you've been seeing is your wife. Your so-called models that you've been fucking are your wife. Hell! While we're at it, that got damn crack pipe is your wife". Suddenly, out of no-where Roscoe punched her so hard that she fell to the floor. By this time the kids had all came out their rooms and was witnessing everything that was going on. Scoe didn't know rather to help his mom who was fighting his dad back or rather to console his siblings who were crying and in an uproar.

Scoe had witnessed many fights that his parents had but for some reason he noticed that this time was different than the rest. He could tell that his dad was seriously out of control and was truly trying purposely to hurt Kelly as he had her pinned down on the floor. Even when she began crying from the physical pain he was causing he had no remorse and just kept on fighting her. As Scoe began to leave the area where the other children were and walk towards his parents, his dad turned with one swift movement and yelled, "take yawl asses to your room." The kids all hurried, frightened by how their dad was acting, but Scoe stood there for another moment. "You too Scoe! Go to your room, your mama alright," he stated knowing that his son was not going to go to his room until he knew she was fine. So, Scoe went upstairs to find all his siblings gathered together in one room.

After a few hours had passed, Kelly called for the children as they came running to see what was going on. "I want you all to pack some of your clothes and things in your book bags because we are leaving in the morning," she said with her eyes overwhelmed with tears. All the children except one began to quickly go and gather their things and do as their mother said. Suddenly, Kelly heard this small voice that nearly broke her heart. Scoe slightly younger brother Ray said, "I'm not leaving, I want to stay here with my daddy." For a brief moment everyone stopped and began to look at one another to see what would happen next. Scoe was burdened by the decision his brother had made. He began to quickly weigh everything in his mind. He came to the conclusion that there was no way he was about to leave his little brother there with their dad to fend for himself. So without another thought being able to enter his mind, Scoe said, "Yea! I don't want to leave either." Kelly could not believe it. Scoe could see the heart in his mom's face and he did not really want to stay there with his dad. He truly, wanted to go with his mother and other siblings. He knew this would be the time when his mom would need him most, but there was no way he was going to run the risk of leaving Ray. Scoe felt that if the other siblings were with Kelly and if he stayed with Ray, then he would undoubtedly know that everyone was safe and secure. It was against Kelly better judgment, and although she was hurt about leaving her two sons behind, she knew that there was no way she and Roscoe could stay in the same house any longer without someone ending up hurt. She didn't want either of them to be there, but she felt a little better in knowing that Scoe would look after Ray and make grown up decisions, the way he always had. So early the next morning; they all said their good-byes.

Once Roscoe realized that his two older sons who were barely teenagers were staying with him, he decided to turn the home into a drug house and have the boys run it. For an entire week Roscoe trained them as if they were on a job site. He taught them how to cook, measure and cut the drugs. He told them to make sure when they always be on the look-out for the police or people who look suspicious. He made sure they knew how to protect themselves by always having a gun in hand when serving customers. After the week of hands-on training, Roscoe felt like they were ready to handle it on their own. Both of the boys were excited about their new lifestyle and the power they felt when they held guns in their young hands. But every so often, Scoe would lay in bed and think of his mother and other siblings. When Saturday rolled around Roscoe popped up to see how the boys were doing and to collect the money they had made, as well as pay them their cut. As they awoke and came downstairs upon hearing their dad's voice, they were shocked at the person he had with him. "Hey! I want yawl to meet someone." Roscoe said as this gay guy stood their acting as bashful as a woman does. "He is going to do all the cooking and cleaning around the house, so Scoe you don't have to do none of that, just focus on bringing in the money," Roscoe stated as he began dividing the money. Neither Scoe nor Ray really wanted a gay guy flaunting around the house but they adhered to their dad orders.

Business really began picking up, and other people who sold drugs in the neighborhood were beginning to get jealous. Everyday something was going on either with them fighting or shooting outside of the house. Scoe knew that this was mainly happening because the other dealers felt like they were only kids and he knew that it wouldn't be like that if his dad was seen at the house more. One day Scoe went into the basement to grab more supplies to cook the drugs and walked in on his dad receiving a blow job from the lady down the street who his mom said he was cheating with all along. He couldn't believe it. Scoe always thought his mother was just going a little over board with the cheating but low and behold she was right. Although Scoe was beginning to witness more and more sides of his dad that he did not like, he couldn't help but enjoy the new level of respect he and Ray was getting on the block and at school. They were able to dress in the finest clothes and top brand sneakers which made Scoe very happy. He began calculating how profit works and put together all sorts of plans on how to make his money increase. The boys were beginning to make plans on how they would be the biggest and most well-known drug dealers in the city. Something that really caused Scoe to become addicted to getting money was when the prettiest girl in school, finally took notice of him. Her name was Jameica Harris and she agreed to be his girlfriend. During this time Scoe stilled played football and everyone in the school loved him. However, things were about to change.

Late one afternoon as Scoe sat at the dining room table there was a knock at the door. He thought it was a customer wanting to be served but it was Ms. Molly from next door. "You have a phone call," she said as Scoe was opening the door and then she walked off the porch. Scoe grabbed his keys off the table, locked the door and proceeded next door to Ms. Molly's house. "Hello," he said while hold the phone to his ear. Relieved to hear his voice, Kelly quickly replied, "I've been trying to reach you for a couple of days now, are you and your brother okay"? Scoe heart melted upon hearing his mother's voice. "Yes!" he stated while staring off into the cream colored ceiling. "Well your uncle is going to come and get you and Ray to take yawl to visit your grandma, so be ready! He should be there soon and you know how he gets," Kelly said. "Okay," Scoe replied as they hung up the phone and he thanked Ms. Molly and went back to his house.

By the time he told Ray what was going on and they grabbed a few things to take with them their uncle was outside blowing the horn. The boys ran out and climbed into the back of the car. As time passed, Scoe began to look out the window of the car. "Geesh! This is a long ride," he thought to himself. Then they finally pulled up at a big building. "Where are we?" Scoe asked as he looked around. "Just come on," his uncle replied with a straight face. Suddenly, it clicked, once he read the big sign on the top of the building that said Haven Domestic Abuse Shelter. Kelly came out to meet them. Scoe was having mixed feelings about everything that was going on. Although he was happy to see everyone, he couldn't believe his mother lied about where they were going, didn't give them a choice and the fact that their uncle was actually in on the kidnapping. What he didn't know was that Roscoe had called Kelly's mom and asked her to get in contact with Kelly and have her to get the boys for him because he knew he wasn't raising them well. Kelly knew if she had told Scoe what was really going on that he would have stayed, just to prove that he was man enough to run the house. However, the only thing that Scoe knew was that the lifestyle that he had grown accustomed to was now over.

He thought about the fact that this was the end of his eighth grade year and how he wouldn't get to graduate with the rest of his classmates. He reminisced on how he was finally able to wear the top named brand shoes and clothes. The confidence he had finally got to bravely talk to any girl he liked. He thought about Jameica Harris and how she was finally his girlfriend after having a crush on her for three years. But most of all he thought of his football team. The one thing that made him feel like he belonged, the discipline and motivation he received from the coaches and the loyalty and respect the players showed one another. He had plans on becoming the star running back for Kettering High School, but now all hopes were gone. Scoe became furious! But he had way too much respect for his mother to show it outwardly. He couldn't understand why when it seemed like everything would be going great then all would be lost and they had to start over again. He did not want to meet new people, he didn't want to attend a new school and by all means he hated being in a shelter. He slowly became numb, the more days they spent in the shelter. Scoe began to develop a detachment from hope, because he now felt like everything would eventually fall through the cracks. The beauty of childhood had been fully stripped from him and his heart was beginning to run cold.

Roscoe was also having a hard time coping with everything that was going on. He had got even heavier off into drugs, to try and erase the memory of all the bad choices he had made. Later within the year, part of the house caught on fire. Moses heard what was going on and came over to see about his friend. Upon noticing that Roscoe was living in a house without any heat or electricity in the dead of winter, he offered for him to come and live with him, but Roscoe refused. "I'll be fine, the neighbors are allowing me to use some of their power until I get mines back on," he said while pointing down at the cords that ran out the side window over to the neighbor's house. The two of them sat there in the house smoking and talking for hours. "Kelly and the kids mean everything to me, and now they're gone. She took my world from me," Roscoe said as he passed the joint to Moses. "You'll be okay, just hang in there," Moses replied. However, deep down he could feel Roscoe was truly hurting inside.

Chapter 7
Distance

By this time Scoe and his family were doing much better. For the first time in his life, Scoe began to see the hustler inside his mom come out. She found a house for her and the kids in Pontiac, MI and worked in the shelter across the street as a crisis counselor. She made sure that her family was well taken care of and that they lived a life that was comfortable and safe. Things were really beginning to look brighter and Scoe decided that he would make the best of his new area. Because of his outgoing personality, he made friends in the neighborhood quickly.

However, he found them to be much different from the type of people he was use to hanging around. These kids pretty much got along with one another and were more polite and friendly. Scoe was eager to find out where he could play football in his new city; so he began to ask around until he found out where to go. Upon signing up for the team and being accepted, it seemed like everything was picking up where it left off, but this time even greater. Especially considering Scoe was now in high school, he knew that colleges would be looking at his football skills and there would be a good chance of him getting scholarships. With this in mind, he was determined to play the sport to the best of his ability and give it all he had. Once again everyone quickly fell in love with his skills at football and he quickly became the star running back for the team. Along with him helping them to win trophies and medals he was invited to attend several social events, which was very new to him.

He enjoyed the functions and met a lot of really nice people, mentors and the prettiest girls he ever saw. However, nothing was more passionate to him than spending time on the field. Then one evening as he sat at home watching television with his siblings there was a knock at the door. Scoe still had the protective character about himself so he told the rest of the kids he would answer it. "Who is it?" he yelled while walking towards the front of the house. To his surprise it was an answer he was not at all prepared to hear. "It's your daddy," Roscoe said while standing on the front porch. Scoe could not believe his ears. How did he find them? What did he want?

Scoe thought to himself, but he would not open the door. Roscoe steady knocked and then went from window to window. The other kids huddled around wondering what was going to happen next. But Scoe took on another mentality at this point. He felt as though he was not a child anymore and the man inside of him stood up. He knew that Roscoe would only come in and do the same thing all over again and make everybody life miserable and he wasn't buying it. As Scoe looked from the window he saw his mom walk up and she and Roscoe began talking outside. After around fifteen minutes they both preceded to come into the house. Scoe could not believe she let him in. He did not want him there; disrespect and contentment showed in his face towards Roscoe. While the other children and Kelly was in there talking with Roscoe, Scoe was preparing for the worst. He had a pole prepared for use and would undoubtedly use it, the moment that Roscoe laid one finger on his mother.

The other children eventually went off to bed, while Roscoe and Kelly stayed up talking. However, Scoe was not about to go to sleep until he knew what was going on.

He listened to their conversation and how his dad began telling Kelly that he was about to get money from the house and how his life was about to change for the better. He went on to say that he was going to do right by her and the kids this time and all he needed was for her to give him a chance. He spoke of promises that they would be like they were when they first met and she wouldn't have to want for anything. As Kelly went on listening to Roscoe speak, Scoe was saying to himself, "Mama please don't fall for this; you've heard all these lies before." But he didn't say one word or let them know he was eavesdropping. He quietly listened and waited to see what Kelly response was going to be. Scoe knew that his dad loved all his children but because of everything he learned growing up selling drugs and the things he witnessed drug addicts do, he knew that Roscoe would be capable of giving compassion to anyone as long as he was on drugs.

Finally Kelly spoke, "I tell you what Roscoe, you go and get the money from the house and then we'll talk about you coming back." Kelly replied with a straight face. Scoe wished his mom would have thrown him out and said never come back. However, her current response was enough for him as he watched her let him out the door and locked it behind him.

As weeks went by; everyone continued throughout their daily routines as usual. It was as if Roscoe had never stopped by. Kelly was doing great at her job and maintaining a steady income that kept her and the children in a good financial state. Scoe was steadily making tremendous progress with the football team and loved how his life was going. Being introduced to this lifestyle where even the teenagers did things with class and respect was just what he needed to become balanced in society. One evening he sat at the table in the dining room of their home and began to look through some of the pictures he had of the team winning their games. Although Kelly was still unavailable to attend any of his games, Scoe purposed in his heart that one day he was going to make her proud, by becoming an NFL legend. As he slowly glanced over at the clock he saw that it was getting late and he hadn't finished cleaning the kitchen, so he began gathering the pictures and putting his things away in his room. As he was headed towards the kitchen there was a knock at the door. "Who is it?" he yelled while walking through the living room towards the front door. "It's your daddy, open the door," Roscoe said from the other side. "No, I can't let anyone into the house," Scoe replied as he walked over to grab the telephone. He called over to the shelter and told his mom that Roscoe was outside at the door. "Yeah, I'm watching him from my office. I'm on my way," she said as she put her coat on and proceeded towards the house. Scoe looked out the window and watched as his mother and fathers met up on the sidewalk and begin talking. He could hear his dad asking Kelly why he wouldn't open the door for him. "He's only being obedient to what he was informed," Kelly stated in an authoritative tone. "Well, I understand if he doesn't open the door for strangers, but I'm his father! There should be no questions about letting me in," Roscoe replied.

Kelly ignored the situation and watched as Scoe went into the kitchen to finish cleaning. "Would you like a cup of water," Kelly asked as she walked towards the kitchen. "Yeah! I will take a glass," Roscoe replied. However,

Kelly just wanted to go where Scoe was to give him instructions on what she witnessed from her office. "I don't know what your daddy is up too, but he hid a gun underneath the back porch when he was outside knocking. I want you to sneak out the back door and get it. Hide it in your room so in case something happens, he can't get to it", she whispered softly while pouring both her and Roscoe a glass of water. Upon her returning back into the living room, Scoe waited a couple of minutes and did as his mother instructed him. Thoughts ran through his mind as he wondered why his dad would bring a gun over and then hide it. What was he up too? Scoe came back into the kitchen and finished his chores.

    He then sat at the dining room table and pretended to be doing his homework, but really so that he might listen in on the conversation. "So did you get the money from the house?" Kelly asked while staring at Roscoe. "Baby, let me tell you what happened; I got the money for the house right, but the banks and everybody were giving me a hard time, so the people told me to get the church to help me get it and they helped me get it but they ended up keeping all of it," Roscoe replied as he continued drinking his water. "The church kept all your money," Kelly asked in doubt of his story being true. "Yes all of it! What you don't believe me or something?" Roscoe asked with that familiar look of rage in his eyes and within his tone of voice. Scoe quickly looked up from the table into the living room where they were. He was prepared this time to defend his mother at all cost, so he rose up from the table and walked towards them. "Daddy, don't come out here with that Shit!" Scoe yelled as he came closer. Neither Kelly nor Roscoe could believe that he actually cussed at him, but Kelly knew that her son was just as much fed up with the nonsense as she was, so she didn't say one word about him disrespecting Roscoe.

"Oh! You gone just stand there and let him talk to me like he grown?" Roscoe yelled while grabbing and yanking Kelly by the arm that he had injured years ago. As the two of them began tussling back and forth, Scoe knew where the night was heading so he quickly thought to call the police and then joined with his mother to fight Roscoe.

Due to the area that they live in, the Pontiac Police Dept. response time was twice as fast as that of Detroit. So they were there before things got really bad. As they began to separately question Kelly and Roscoe, Scoe went over to console his other siblings who had been awakened by the commotion. As he occasionally glanced into the living room, he could tell by the look on his mother face that she was not very pleased with what they were saying. "There's nothing we can really do, because there are no signs of abuse or forced entry," the officer said while writing on his notepad. "You don't understand! There has to be some way you can help me. Me and my children lives are in danger if you leave him here with me," Kelly proclaimed with tears rolling down her face. The officer could see the sincerity in her eyes and slowly glanced over as Scoe and his siblings were huddled in the other room. His heart was moved with compassion as he said, "Okay, we cannot arrest him but we can detain him for a while." That's all Kelly needed to hear as she had already made up in her mind that they were going to leave while he was at the police station. As soon as the officers put Roscoe in the car and pulled off, Kelly came running through the house yelling for the children to grab some of their things so they could leave. All of them began to do as they were told, but Roscoe stood there for a moment. "Where are we going? The police have him now, so we should be fine right?" he asked while staring at his mother as she quickly gathered some things to take with them. "Scoe, I don't have time to discuss this right now, just grab some of your stuff, we have to go! They didn't arrest him they can only detain him for so long and then they will release him," Kelly replied. Scoe was very upset that they had to be on the run again, but he was even angrier when he realized that after the long drive to Mt. Clemens, MI., they were about to spend the night in another shelter.

Chapter 8
Shadows

After being in the shelter for a couple of days; Scoe wondered how long this process was going to last. He was eager to get back to school and be around his friends. He missed having the privacy of their own home and being able to go in the kitchen and get a snack whenever he felt like it. Spending time in a shelter always made him feel belittled, restricted and defeated. Then one day his mom gathered them all together and told them that they were leaving. Scoe and the children all began to get excited. They couldn't wait to get back to life as they knew it. They were all eager to be within their level of comfort and enjoyment. However, what Kelly told them next, caused all of them except Scoe, to be filled with confusion, excitement and worry at the same time. "We are moving to Clarksdale, Mississippi with grandpa," she said in her sweet motherly voice.

Upon hearing this, Scoe was furious. He felt that his dreams had been deferred again. How could this be happening he began to think? He didn't fully know what was running through the minds of his brothers and sisters nor did he know how they really felt about the situation, but he knew without a shadow of doubt, he did not want to be uprooted again. He thought about how far he had come in playing football. Truly, his team would be devastated upon hearing that they were going to lose the captain of the team. He would have to break the heart of another young lady who had been his girlfriend for over a year now. What would he say to her? So many thoughts ran through his mind that he could barely contain himself. However, he continued to pack his things like the rest of the children.

Upon reaching their destination Scoe realized that they were not the only family members who were staying with his grandfather. He and his six siblings shared the living room as sleeping quarters, along with a few of their cousins. At grandpa house everyone had to be up early in the mornings to get the day started. There were no ifs, and, or buts about it. So every morning after they arose, prepared for the day and ate breakfast, Scoe would then go outside and take a walk. He needed his alone time to think and try to clear his mind from allowing negativity to take over. He really missed his friends in Michigan and didn't know how long Kelly had planned to stay in Mississippi.

One day he stopped at a nearby park and sat on the bench and began to watch the people as they passed by. Everyone seemed to be so very country to him and he just couldn't understand why he always had to adapt to new environments. "Is this some cruel joke?" he whispered under his breath in speaking directly to God. "This can't be the way life is supposed to go! I know you have something better for me than this," he continued to pray in a low toned voice, so that people wouldn't think he'd gone crazy. Scoe felt so disappointed that he began to walk some more to avoid giving up all together. He trusted that God was going to make everything okay, as always.

However, the pressure was putting a strain on his faith and relationship with God. As he kept walking, he found a football team out practicing. He became excited for a moment, but when he inquired about joining them, the head coach informed him that he was too late and they were already at the end of the season. However, the coach saw the disappointment in his eyes and allowed him to practice with them anyway. Scoe began to loosen up a little and became more comfortable about being out of state, since he had found to do something he enjoyed. His faith began to increase again, and he felt that God always would make a way.

On the following Wednesday, after practicing with the players, Scoe came back to his grandfather's house tired, but still enthused to be involved with the sport. But to his surprise, when he walked into the house Kelly and the kids were packing. "We're going back home now," she said as Scoe stood there in disbelief. This time he wasn't as upset that they were once again moving because they were going to go back to their house in Pontiac. He knew that he would be with his old friends and also have the opportunity to see his girlfriend and this made him happy.

Upon Kelly arriving back in Michigan, she took the advice she was given and filed a restraining order against Roscoe coming near her and the children. She also filed for a divorce and everything was being processed. After around a year and a half, it seemed like everything was smooth sailing. Roscoe had abided by the laws that were put in place and had not bothered Kelly or the children. However, Kelly never felt really safe or had good-nights rest, with knowing that Roscoe still knew where they lived. So she decided that they would move once more. Scoe pleaded for them to stay and tried to express how important playing football meant to him. He explained how the season had rolled back around and they were winning all their games. But Kelly was not concerned with him playing any sports. She considered their safety to be more of an importance and felt that Scoe could play football anywhere. She never knew how them being unstable was affecting his spirit and causing him to become bitter. He never told her, how his hope for anything was being diminished or how he was beginning to give up on ever being happy or settled in life. Scoe just continued to do as he always would, and followed his mother's orders to see what would come next. So within the next month Kelly moved her family to the north side of Pontiac, MI. Very few people knew where they were and she liked it that way. It made her feel that her and her children were safe.

Two years had gone by and everything was seemingly going fine; until the telephone rang. The kids were all in the house laughing and playing around as usual. Suddenly, Scoe looked up at his mother and noticed that countenance had changed. As she held the phone, her hand began trembling and tears rolled down her sweet face.

Then she said okay and hung up the phone. "Who was that?" Scoe asked as his mother stared off into the corner of the room. "That was your grandmother, she called to tell me that yawl father was killed," Kelly said as she began to cry. Although they had went through a lot of bad times, Kelly never truly stop loving Roscoe.

As the other children cried and were all saddened, Scoe slowly put his head down and moped to the back of the house. However, as soon as he reached his room he closed and locked his door, turned the radio on loudly and then stopped pretending to be sad. Scoe was not sad one bit about the news of his father murder. Instead he was excited! As the song "Can you stand the rain?" played on the radio, Scoe released a big sigh of relief. He finally felt that all the running would cease. He knew that his mom would truly be free from fear and he wouldn't have to be worried day and night anymore about his dad hurting her or wondering if she would be murdered by his hands. Scoe felt a release so strong that he couldn't explain it. He definitely couldn't share how he felt with anyone else either, because they would not understand why he was so happy at a time that everyone else was so sad. But all the years of batter, abuse, rage and negativity had hardened this young man heart to the point where he did not give a damn about what had happened. All the years of balled up anger were now diminished in a matter of seconds.

During the days leading up to the funeral and even the day of the funeral; Scoe did as others and moped around pretending to be grieving. Everything he encountered throughout his childhood ended in ultimate failure and he knew that was primarily due to the lifestyle his dad had chosen. Watching his mother love a man whole heartedly who only tried to hurt her in return, caused a real dark cloud to be in his spirit that he could not shake. Scoe watched his father's side of the family, fervently grieve the loss of Roscoe and yet he still was not moved with compassion. He looked around the room at each of them with no remorse. He thought about the time he overheard his grandmother tell his dad that Kelly needed to get her ass beat from time to time. He wondered if his dad would have been a different person if he had been taught differently. Upon all these thoughts running through his mind, he decided that he wanted nothing to do with Roscoe's side of the family ever again. Deep down Scoe was a little hurt by his father passing away, but knowing the fact that they would now have a life, no more living in shelters or having to be up on patrol all night was more powerful than his sorrow.

Therefore, many years after the day of the funeral, up until this very moment, Scoe has lived a lifestyle that everyone claimed was patterned like that of his father. Even he had seen some similarities arise every so often and try to shake them off. His determination is to never walk in his father's shadows.

Roscoe Copeland
Aka "Scoe"

www.ingramcontent.com/pod-product-compliance
Lightning Source LLC
Chambersburg PA
CBHW071514150426
43191CB00009B/1520